Uncoupling

Uncoupling

Margo Davis

Copyright 2025 @ Margo Davis
All Rights Reserved

ISBN: 978-1-962148-23-8
LOC: 9781962148238

Editor: Rylee Wenzel
Author Photo: John Slaby

Lamar University Literary Press
Beaumont, TX

Acknowledgments

Many of these poems originally appeared in the following journals and anthologies (some with minor changes):

Agave Magazine
Dallas Review
Dead Mule School of Southern Lit
Deep South Magazine
The Ekphrastic Review
Ellipsis
Equinox Biannual Journal
Friendswood Library Ekphrastic Poetry Festival
50 Give or Take
Houston Chronicle
Light Journal
Literature Today
Louisiana Literature
The Louisville Review
Manchac
Maple Leaf Rag
Mockingheart Review
ND Quarterly
Negative Capability: The Big Easy Crescent City That Care Forgot
New Orleans Review
Ocotillo Review
Odes and Elegies: Eco-Poetry from the Texas Gulf Coast
Out of the Depths, Poetry of Poverty—Courage and Resiliene
Passages North
Poetry Quarterly
Quicksilver (Finishing Line Press, 2022)
San Antonio Express-News
Senior Class: 100 Poems on Aging
Snapdragon: A Journal of Art & Healing
Southwest Review
Untameable City: Poems on the Nature of Houston
Verse Daily
Voices de la Luna: Earth in Peril / in Praise
Waco Wordfest
What Rough Beast
Willawaw Journal
WomenArts Quarterly

CONTENTS

ONE

10   Southern Tradition
11   Male Gaze
12   Sunday Worship
13   First One thing, Then Another
14   Fences
15   If Only
16   The Gravity of Flight
17   I withdrew
18   I found him
19   Appetite
20   From Where I Sit
21   Tryst

TWO

24   Weak-kneed
25   Invocation
26   Your light air
27   Crush
28   In the distance
29   What's in the Stars
30   From my dining table
31   Leafcutter Ants
32   Afoot
33   Scaling
34   Your Abrupt Departure
35   Quicksilver
36   Off Schedule
37   I won't
38   Museum Reception
39   Nothing sounds
40   Affect
41   My Kinda Town
42   After-dinner Repast
43   You don't say

THREE

46	Wheel of Misfortune
47	Believe
48	Suburban Tremors
49	Fall
50	I don't say
51	Roughing It
53	Doubt
54	Afterglow
55	I heard
57	Grey Days
58	Better Times
59	Found Footage
60	Middle Child
61	Picnic
63	Dirt Poor
64	Up in Smoke
65	Playing With Fire

FOUR

68	Fire!
69	Heading back from Padre Island
70	Imagine
71	Late Season
72	Fading Light
73	Framed
74	Unrest
75	Detritus
76	Bedside Vigil
78	Man At Work
79	I don't
80	Music of the Spheres
81	A Day So Pleasant
82	Breathless In Portugal

ONE

...never more serious than when joking.

—Robert Frost

Southern Tradition

A Southern woman could
lace a rat with garnish
and pass it on.

A Southern gentleman would
not partake but celebrate
with a story—

enhancing the moldy rat,
redefining it,
until the rat is endearing—

a second cousin, eccentric
but so necessary,
embracing half-truths,

the mixologist's cocktails
upended by the refrain:
hurricane comin'!

Male Gaze

Men were pulled by the moon
while I went to work
at sunrise

and returned in darkness
to that first small step
for mankind.

Male astronauts swooned from
moonlight, cameras.
The lookers,

dreamy and aloof, gazed
into space as men
would pursue,

wobbling. I would scoop up
those on the rebound,
men who slipped.

Sunday Worship

Ray says something about honor
and quiet, here in the Mangrove Swamps,
only I can't hear him for the whirr
of the motor. He must have read my face
for he pantomimes, *what   what?*
I want to tell him there's no sport in
tricking snappers into gillnets, no grace,
but I know this to be trawling
for trouble. Ray worries the waters
among stumps he insists all look alike.
Above swamp fog, a great blue heron lifts
then glides above cattails before
easing me onto safer ground.

First One Thing, Then Another

Not long ago you couldn't get enough
of me. Now it's popcorn—

mountainous heaps of
perfectly popped melt-in-your-mouth
morsels. You're never satisfied.
I munch one or two handfuls, sigh.

Your *good night*, a vague pat
between the chair and my bare knee.

I can't center on my
confusion longer than ten seconds.
Late in the night, I stumble
barefoot across the sticky kitchen tile.

Soon a legion of Dixie bottles
make harsh music beneath the table.

Salt, everywhere I sit on salt.
By moonlight, I study a kernel
changing its shape like a cloud.
Cross-legged, I mime playing

jacks until the moon retires.
Have I changed that much?

Fences

Maybe fifty cattle thunder downhill toward us, wild-eyed,
their dust-covered muscles shifting in hide like a waterbed.

Unbridled drive drowns out shouts as, bewildered, you back up,

putting more stock in their tumult than a barbed wire fence
they will run up against, assuming they survive the ditch.

You waken, briefly, from your assumption we move in unison.

If Only

After dinner settled, we would
squeeze through a local high school's gate
too loosely chained.

On moonless nights we would
rely on muscle memory to guide our strides
along the track.

My finish time varied little,
according to his stopwatch. I could gauge
how far ahead he ran when

his right foot scuffled pebbles.
By lap seven, about two hundred yards ahead.
That last spring I would slow

on the eighth curve to track
warblers in a cluster of live oaks then make up
for lost time on the ruler-keen

straightaway. Rough breathing,
wild pulse, all I could hear, what and how
I felt. At the finish line

he always lingered, pacing.
I could shave off six or eight seconds,
he would start in,

if only I'd trim the last curve.
If only I'd stay in lane one, he'd continue,
slinging sweat from his brow.

Did I want to run among
those trees? I kept my head cocked for one
bird of encouragement.

The Gravity of Flight

From my unlit apartment I peer
through slits in the blinds.
                               Where are all the joggers?
A foot advances from the shadows

into a lamp post's light
                               then a tiny dog
bounding to keep up with a long gait.

                       Stiffly I fidget, pace.

Even a weary nag called to the barn
can entertain an impulse to fly,

quick as a wink, a twitch,
                               to lift weight and worry and woe,
however short-lived.
                       A difficult win

a hundred fifty years ago when Muybridge,
the motion studies photographer,

documented all four taut legs floating above ground
at once, none touching down.

I withdrew

when love grabbed me from behind
to pose for that photo-friendly hug,

his grip tight, a clumsy wrestle
we each knew no sure sign of

affection. I could sense how he felt
pressed to assure the others, *I am*

here, we are fine. He doubled for
my mother's clammy hover,

mimed grimace immortalizing
on film how we should be.

Her pantomime, choking me
from behind. Rough, too long held

against my will, without warning,
no hint of sloppy endearment.

Even as a child I knew I served
to prop her up, a slight shield

against what might be slung.
Perhaps mere diversion to fill her

void. All those long silences
endured as she drew energy for

just such awkward moments. So
too this elusive man's embrace

I shunned, stunned. I didn't want
—I didn't need—that touch.

I found him

baffling as an eye chart.
Often removing my glasses
to wipe them
not with his shirttail
or a cloth napkin
but with a clean kerchief.
There are worse traits
so I smiled my thanks.
Could I see
any difference? All a blur
til surgery. I'd been burdened
with smudges, partial prints,
impurities a windshield
will endure until wipers
bring relief. Maybe
as I groped I should have
asked, how dirty *are*
my glasses? Maybe,
what color are my eyes?
No. Yours? Really,
I want to know, could he
no longer tolerate
a messy world? My world?
I would ask, *is that why
you disappeared*? I can see
now. I have depth.
I see he's gone.

Appetite

I wander the dim-lit neighborhood to watch
how others socialize. Up the block
lilting dinner party guests gather,
drinks in hand.
Every so often someone breaks
then glides toward another tight cluster.
A female tilts her head, listening intently
while a man boasts
over another's squared shoulder. A woman
studies the carpet. Is it hers?
Does she have carpet
envy, too? Is this somebody's husband
hers? Emphatically he drills a point lost on her.
Chatting women throw back their heads,

laugh. She startles.
The hostess—too smartly dressed to be wait-staff—
advances with a tray of nibbles
I can't quite taste. She makes eye contact,
adroitly urging a napkin
into a guest's palm. This does the trick.
Tidbits float from tray to hand outstretched.
Smooth. I mimic her poise
beneath a valanced window, my hip swishing
my imaginary Donna Reid skirt
draped in moonlight the color of whiskey,
neat. Then pirouette, tray extended,
offing, *Do try this*.

From Where I Sit

Her Bloody Mary spots her spandex,
a pool of red on white. Soft laughter.
Her Anthony leans across for a hot roll,
tears it slowly to study steam,
then presses the warm loaf to her stained leg,
teasing the spot dry.

Oh my.

When her hand gropes for a water glass,
I suspect she'll cool her pants
or douse his eager face. But no,
she pours on her lap a fresh wet spot,
an invitation for him to wipe
what she made wet.

What relief,

there is no bread. He mouths,
waiter, tucks napkin beneath a plate
as if linen were her bodice,
her skin porcelain. She mouths *oh* or *no*
(eyes saying more from where I sit)
and the two slip out the door.

Tryst

I'm smoke off the grill,
spidery tingle on the wrist.

Feel the swoop of wings.
Over the fence, a faint sigh.

Does your backbone shift?
In your body an ache must stir.

Caress me. Listen,
I whisper softly, *let's fix this*.

This is my art. My lips
linger, part. An illusion mixes

grit with bliss. Oh, reaching
out? What an injurious hex.

Shrug. Still elusive?
Lean in. Just one vexing kiss.

TWO

My study is a kind of laboratory. Like all experiments, some succeed and others fail.

—Pablo Picasso

Weak-kneed

Is there a word for aching
for the imagined?

His arm sweeps the back of my chair,
hand lightly brushing my

shoulder, arm. I shudder. How I yearn

to be his lover,
not that coarse woman accustomed to

his attention. Flushed,

I must excuse myself
to find myself in the bathroom mirror.

Returning

I spot a lash on his cheek—

his? hers?—

Maybe
maybe I'll lean in   blow softly

when she scrapes it off
as if peeling wax from linoleum.

Invocation

*golden shovel using a line from
Terrance Hayes' "The Same City"*

A cathedral hush within &
then a crushing force more holy

than I merit. I perspire as
this power whooshes within, the

light filling as his gentle mouth
draws near, nearer, a soft breath of
want above my upper lip. An

abundant ache belies infant-
ile hunger for his kiss. Heart, it

upends heaven's redemption. Is
this holy? No? Lord. I'm speechless.

Your light air

buoyed my vested heart. Here we navigate
unknown waters
along the shallows.

I want

to backstroke to our past before wading
into a murky now.
You glide, effortless,

then back

paddle, leaning far in, gently brushing my
breast, flailing arm
coaxing me, *Relax.*

Now float.

Crush

I go half crazy, interludes
so brief I develop shortness of breath
around you,

who know my breath, yours,
yours mine

until we two grow heady
waiting, wanting, wooing. My breath
wheezing, I

fall faint as I feign the wait
worth the weight

on my ribcage you take
care not to crush yet do nonetheless.
We accordion.

In the distance

I see a bustling chicken shack. Further,
the two-lane tumbles, waiting. Still no you. From here,

boat slips and a lake house. I wait uphill
among dappled rooftops. Wrong way. Turn south from here.

My heart quickens when cars lurch southward or
flocks overhead wait in V formation. From here

their route south makes me want to sprout feathers.
I'd sooner walk home than wait. What's today? From here

I imagine you wait. Please, keep busy.
A car backfires. I wonder, no, worry, from here

that some lovely woman will catch your gaze.
From a low curvy limb a dove woos, waits. From here

I wait, counting long moments. Miles lengthen.
Time potholes the unlit wavy blacktop. From here

my pulse gyrates. Heaven's gate scrapes my rear.
No straight shot awaits. There's no shortcut, dear, from here.

What's in the Stars

I stir when I feel fingertips
along my forearm—

then find myself alone in bed so far from

your embrace. Do you now cuddle
another? Mirror

fiery eyes? Notes scrawl across a solemn sky,

die. Oh! Brittle copper lightning
flashing eight, nine times,

perhaps seven, no, eight, aiming for the heart

whose every steadfast beat I
for so long counted,

counted on. Now glinting stars pulsate, *so long*.

From my dining table

I glance out the window
overlooking the neighbor's perennial

attempts. Anemic leaves
tap along our wooden fence meant to keep
others out, me within.

Pale colors could soothe
though I would pluck them by the handfuls,

whittle every branch,
high then low— to have you here again,
igniting the horizon

with your candlelit eyes
that draw me in, hypnotize, as I follow
wherever. Set me afire.

Leafcutter ants

keep in lockstep on the curb, one then another to the furthest tip
    of an orderly world.

To the casual eye, each similar enough, with the same movements,
    an even pace, no

hesitation. What purpose in their progress, hundreds or thousands
    threading through

the same-colored growth. Camouflage, were it not for flouncing
    each prize. What

distinguishes one from another? The leaf each fashions like a sail,
    celadon to mint.

One, blushing pink. More like Sunday hats. Outlandish. In a wind,
    their mandibles

lock down on the ragged morsel. Each shimmering overblown fan
    three times taller

than the spindly efficient vessel that conquers a stiff blade of grass,
    hard pebble, a path

curving ever so slightly. Never letting up. Admirable. Humbling.
    Near maniacal!

And when on impulse I reach over and remove one little insect's
    booty, not to be

cruel but empirical, the ruffled creature tips sideways, lightheaded.
    Its stagger breaks

a follower's lockstep. The scientist within repositions the morsel
    onto the panicked

ant now tussling over another's floppy leaf. Next the stripped ant
    retraces its steps.

Afoot

Why say no, why,
when your eyes plead, please?
Do you lean in

or is it me? Your hand reaches out
to embrace my cheek.

Or do you mean to
smooth out more frown lines—
my confusion?

You hover over your chair then
shoot up, pulling me into

an embrace I match.
Afterward, an absentminded peck
lands and lights,

a butterfly in flight. When
in public, as others flit and flutter,

your mettle, lackluster,
head pulling back. Stunned pupils,
crushed metal.

Scaling

Beckoning to follow,
the taut mountaineer shoots up a
rusty circular metal stairwell of half-steps
fashioned by Dr. Seuss. I cling to this damp railing then
trip on the third-floor landing. *How much further
to my room?* I pant. The local legend
says evenly, *Plan the next
step. Only that.*

Your Abrupt Departure

Cooled candle wax.
Pile of burnt matches, whiff of sulfur.

Salt lacing the plate,
cork wedged in the neck you would

absently rub. Your door
key found near the front door whose

knob would shiver
at your touch. Dawn light stretches

heel to toe, yawning.
Indented throw pillow waiting it out.

Quicksilver

When I find myself
reaching up to brush away

the curl teasing your eyelash—
mere reflex— you pull back.

We both note your body
refusing to be swayed

by me. Our wordless
exchange, a standoff.

This moment, the last
rapturous air we share.

I hold my breath. You
inhale evenly, intact.

Off Schedule

Another restless night in bed
and still no heat.

The Union Pacific pants somewhere in the distance—
departing or oncoming?

That would depend, I guess,
on whether I'm asleep.

Feet root for last night's socks
as the train ricochets, a tipsy caboose venturing home.

A potbelly moon exhales
vapors. This icy boxcar room,

dark as pitch. A humming power line tethers me in place.
My electric blanket, stripped

of cords, switches. My
big toe chugs through a hole

in its satin hem. Do I dream
a frayed wire set the mattress afire? Rolling directly onto

its furnace, my knees flew up
to sooth my wild heart.

The calving train now clanks side to side, lowing. Limbs,
unspring, stretch stiff as tracks.

Locomotive, scorch the rails.
Rock me back to sleep.

I won't

Am I fawning when
I apologize

for the pain I still
wrestle with? I persist,

hounding you, don't I,
reframing, re-

membering, re-
shaping your part.

Oh conflicted Heart,
what yearning,

that petal soft tone
an art. We can't, no.

Museum Reception

Furtively I scan for
some sign he remembers
that give I still want
from him.
My fingertips tingle
as he travels a hallway
lined with Redon
wallflower friends.
His gaze,
inward.
My eyes trace cheeks
I mustn't touch,
look away. A smile
intended for me?
Words petal,
fall. I yearn to
untangle chest hairs
thick as underbrush.
I am drawn
I confess to this
Adonis who pairs off with
his mirror image.

Nothing sounds

like a tin can rolling down the street
except its mate,

wanting to be stopped. A breeze lifts
sandwich paper,

gives tin a tumble. What a sound!
How can a small

cylinder echo so? Nightfall douses
sharp corners.

Tall dark overlords carry well-lit
gas cans and

whisper into unpeopled buildings,
fire! fire!

Fluorescent lighting on the fritz
pining to be

quarter-moon someday, some
cloudless night.

Dust swivels through corridors
growing bored

by infrequent winds. Alley stains
at sunrise.

Affect

Nervous chatter
to delay the expected moist kiss.
G'bye. No, thanks.
                      Just friends.

Moments husked, blown. Leisure has its way
with poor timing.
                      What happened
to those years between love for another
and another's love for a me
I can't be,

day or night. Never in daylight.
Waiting while keeping busy has kept me
from being.
                      Productivity,
overrated. What's the draw in back-to-back
engagements?
                      Odd couplings.
Short-term commitments cut ongoing issues
into bite sizes.
                      What do the stats
say? Men live longer if married. Mercy,
quality is strained.

My Kinda Town

Lake Michigan, the taxi driver proclaims
with a flourish of his left arm, the cab drifting
into the powdery right lane. Slowing,
he turns a one-eighty in his seat,
his full-on gaze saying, aren't you two
beautiful. There, he points to the perilous
iced-over lake. Or mega-parking lot. The car careens left,
left, hugging the curb. It's what,
barely ten a.m. On we drift among white discs
to a major exhibit at their Art Institute,
its top, saltine-white, on our right.
So soon?
Only four blocks from the hotel?
Could we have trudged our way through
this whiteout? The museum,
shouldering pushy winds. Impromptu he trills
Chi—ca—go!
weaving too close to a neighboring taxi
whose driver honk-prods him over.
The two comrades gesture vaguely, referencing something.
A grudge? The other fare, a couple
quaking, pupils rolled back, mouths agape.
I count altogether ten fillings
as we very nearly cymbal crash. The woman's palms
spread across her window as if pleading,
what, to stop? Let her out? We speed
then slow, sway then swoop far too close to them,
retreat, right, left, squaring off
on awfully thin ice.

After-dinner Repast

My little Pompano, he whispered.
Did I look broad and flat?

He touched me carefully
as though my dry fins would flake

and fall. He would not lift
his gaze to discover I am mermaid,

equal fins and perfection.
Cautiously he braced for the unruly

bone, a filet in his heart.

You don't say

you're sorry. You call
to say you're sorry you didn't call.

Your idea of sorry
is to call and remain silent,
exhaling into the phone.

You're sorry,
you now admit, that you didn't
speak on the first four tries.

I counted six
but perhaps others dialed. Others
weary of words?

This gives me pause.

It was a misstep when I
accepted your exhale by inhaling,

a form of buddy breathing. Only
we aren't buddies. I hope

you quit. Calling.
Exhaling. Believing I will breathe.

I am holding my breath.

THREE

Anybody who has survived his childhood has enough information to last him the rest of his days.

—Flannery O'Connor

Wheel of Misfortune

Out of love you can speak with straight fury.
  —Eudora Welty

As my tanked future ex
stepped from his white Caddy,
the dick threw his Moby in reverse.
All those idling neighbors
saw him T-boning my side door.
God of Mirth, were you outdone?
Oh, Big Wheel, Misfortune,
asleep at some other deal?
Welcome back.
What you drive home I cannot
take to the bank. A bankrupt heart
withdraws little. The candy apple red
replacement panel leans
on crooked door number three,
a locked entry to our basement
of suspect odors. Beyond that door,
Oh, Mr. Price Is Not Right,
a fridge weeps coolant
alongside a forsaken baby grand
with a slack pedal rod.

Believe

Little spark of madness...
you mustn't lose it.
  —Robin Williams

I strive for that
technique learned in acting class
when I palm an ice pick
and glide through shadows.

Strasberg's method
seeks a universal. I strive for
the plight of a spurned woman
getting even. Any wife

would become enraged
if her cohabiting husband became
engaged. I'm actress and
character in one.

Revenge: I inhale, hold,
coil, strike. With a nod to De Niro—
I stab stab again. No, I'll
not pay for custom tires.

Suburban Tremors

I lilt and drop through a hilly neighborhood
where others play overwrought need on wide-screen

bay windows. Anything resembling my past life
I pass by quickly. No need for reruns. I linger instead

for pitches that drift from a slack-jawed window,
a cello moaning low then lower, each vaulted groan

barely clearing the stiff lip of trembling glass
upstairs. Each note scuffs, pretending it doesn't hurt

one bit as it scrapes and grates the pavement
then tumbles into an unmade bedful of damp weeds.

Fall

Pewter light sputters from
a lamppost onto the driveway.

And that mysterious rustle,
a slicker? The eyesore neighbor,

a hoarder, whose meaty thighs
rub together in a tarpaulin sweat.

Flabby arms jiggle and chafe
against his laboring ribcage.

The skeptical moon tracks
his every move at a distance.

There's no sign just yet of
the omniscient black cat slinking

from one dark sinkhole into
the next. A furtive possum

tiptoes across a splintered
backyard fence. Now the man

inches toward my expansive
bay window, his pained face

awash in tonight's news.
Is his internet down? Again?

When he steps on my mislaid
rake, the two go tête-à-tête.

I don't say

I'm sorry when you call
to say you're sorry
that I didn't.

My idea of sorry
is to recall I remained silent,
exhaling with a moan.

I am sorry,
I admit, now that you've quit
pleading. Four times.

I counted six
but perhaps I exaggerate.
Leery of me? You

have cause—
it was a mistake when I
expected to breathe in sync,

a form of coupling. Only
we aren't a couple. I know
you are separate.

I sense your every breath.

Roughing It

While reading on a secluded bench
in a seaside botanic garden

I hear a muffled wheezing then its echo.
One-two.

Its origin, so low to the ground
I assume someone lay curled around a knee-high shrub.

After a few rounds
I venture forward. It stops.

One.
Two.

One-two.   I venture
beyond the bush

to find another one-two angle.
The muffled sound comes from
a cluster of mature pines on a lower-level one-two path.

Three.

What I see is a muscular man
pummeling one-two-three
with his oversized boxing gloves

a tree trunk aproned with a fluffy patterned pillow.
To avoid bruising one-two.

Himself, I wonder, or the tree?

He may get sore one-two-three
but won't bleed
in Mickey Mouse hand-me-downs.

Spindly legs one-two-three hold him up.
Is he driven by a coach's directive,

Hard! Harder!

Perhaps he roughs up nature to cushion his Minnie when he one-two returns home.

Three.

Doubt

Back into
the unexplored darkness, cool, amorphous,

all depth, vaulted ceiling. There's no edge.
It engulfs.

You're unsure
what anchors you here as you teeter a bit,

tremble when a damp breeze stirs the hairs
on your neck.

Whose exhale?
To glance back says goodbye to cascading

light and hello to who or what. Anticipate.
This dank spot

caskets air.
How better to note the low wattage horizon?

Lay yourself bare to whatever you imagine
you flee from.

Afterglow

Never think you've seen the last of anything.
　　　　—Eudora Welty

Your eyes are diamonds, voice gravelly as rust,
as you promise to stay in touch, only this proves too much.

Years have passed since we discussed why I fell out of love—
too painful for either of us. Ah, memories

make fools of us.

We knew our love was a plus. For both of us.
Yet here you are kicking up a fuss. Diamonds and lust.

Hunger made this hard on us. You say I made you
ill but you were always that way. Stardust abrades my trust.

I Heard

quiet, nothing but,
as snow blanketed the spare lawns,
the streets,
even the railroad ties

that glinted and winked like
gold teeth beneath off-white slush
as our lumbering beige car
eased over the tracks.

I would lie awake, hearing
nothing, not even a passing flatbed,
until the 10:45
shimmied and blew through.

At 10:50 our neighbor
would cast a shadow down his stairs
as if in a silent film
then coast his old wreck downhill

until it coughed into being
at bottom, turning left beyond the rails,
arriving on time,
it would seem,

for his 11 o'clock shift
at *The Red White and Brew*.
I heard if you fed quarters to the jukebox
it would play 'til first light.

Some drank there,
I suppose, to blast out thought,
simply be. Perhaps a pounding rhythm
served as prelude or

soundtrack for something
you made happen. Or happened to you.
If I had been drinking age

I would have trudged back home
through the mute snow

simply to process all I had heard.
Back then, I had thought
I'd seen everything.

Grey Days

after Helen Levitt's "Seven Young Boys"

It's black and white, this snapshot
I can't shake off. Young boys,
ranging five to eight, I would guess
not from their heights, exactly,

wafer-thin, in smudged shirts
ragged as the crumbling curb
they idle near. One tyke stands

in the garbage-strewn gutter
as a neighbor boy pedals
a dented tricycle into what seems
a mirror at the center of

the grimy sidewalk. It's 1940,
post-Depression, before the war.
What sorcerer props up this

illusion? A frame minus its mirror,
no reflection, unadorned life itself,
the kid living in reality. At his back,
Walter Quay Hand Laundry.

In his sights, a cohort on the street.
Mere boys, too young for the draft,
caught between causes.

Better Times

The old codger on the adjoining farmland
with the abandoned mine shaft

   (why are mine shafts never boarded up?)

has threatened to shoot Lassie for trespassing

but now the farmer's panicked sister stumbles
in there for her missing kitten—

and then the entrance collapses, dust rising up.
They're trapped in the mine shaft!

   (*Quick!* the collie barks, *Quick! Quick!*)

But before Timmy can leave the kitchen

table, he must finish his meal.
The family looks on as Timmy angles

that three-foot glass of milk.
Lassie pauses while Timmy downs it

   (without wiping his mouth on a sleeve).

Found Footage

Rare sepia clips thread into a projector
propped atop dusty old books.

Tribesmen cloaked in white run barefoot
across a gritty shifting desert,
                        sinking
                        more than moving forward,

each searing stride natural as breath.

        Our first theatre:
        I wore a black velvet A-line dress
        with a thin pink ribbon sash.

Are they fleeing?

Neither terror nor anguish in eyes flecked with cauterizing sunlight.

        Sir Lawrence had camels.
        Where are theirs?

Their need to move, palpable.
                        Toward what?
                                        From what?
        I fidget.
        My Mary Janes slip off.

Their bare ankles sink deeper. Can they move?

The desert shift-and-shimmer coats dark eyes, darker lashes.
Wavy terrain hypnotizes.

        So thirsty.
        Our treat: ice-cold Coca-Cola.

Coarse grains abrade time itself, deflecting the sun's glint.

I lick my lips, dab my brow, swallow.
                        Water.
                              Now.

Middle Child

Here I stand, spirited first grader,
hand on hip, in a black and white photo
familiar as memory.

My uniform collar peeks out
to reveal cherry-blueberry snow cone spills.

I half-recall more mishaps as I
come across another shot, my sister when a
toddler. Cute snowsuit.

Her furry hood's fallen back,
right leg stretched sideways on the bleachers

facing St. Mary's playing field
where our brother defends his middle school
turf, his tribe.

To save face, he scowled at me
all winter as if I were the garish sun itself.

Her soft blond
curls coaxed smiles. There,
that spectral shadow, our Mother Superior

curating a sibs cheering squad
with a boxy Brownie camera. Her cigarette

ashes cracking ice
beneath her insulated boots,
evidence of another cold spell endured.

Picnic

My brother fishtailed along the gravel,
he and Dad debating the perfect tree along the lake,
until Dad yelled,
HERE.

As they untied the trunk,
my new friend and I lined up like leaf ants
to pass fried chicken, potato salad, flaky biscuits,
and an icy watermelon
keeping Dad's cold beer upright in the cooler.

Each barking orders as we giggled
behind fanned-out hands, rolling our eyes.

My birthday cake above our heads,
we swiped a dollop of gooey chocolate until
one of us dropped it —icing first—

in the coarse stones crunching underfoot.
We froze as if hearing, *Simon Says.*

When my brother lopped off pebbled icing,
blessing the cake like Father McGregor,
we fell into giggles.

Dad muttered, wasted store-bought,
adding to his list:
double night shift,
damn kid –

then paused to look across the lake as if
our mother would float back.
Dad refused to eat, downing more beer,

bottles clanking and rolling toward the water,
then he bowled our melon
at the tree, its trunk only slowing the inevitable
plop

into the murky lake,
splitting into halves that bobbed and drifted
around the bend.

My brother disappeared through the trees.
Dad veered home as we pouted in the back seat
over our losses—

icing, watermelon.

Dirt Poor

The lake is really a slate roof.
A duck gliding across the smooth surface
is a plastic bag gulping hot air.
The duck's path, a power line gone slack.
If I squint, my shadow forms a storm cloud,
the whiff of creosote forecasts rain
and that strewn hubcap rap-tapping
across the pock-marked highway, music
for my tapping foot. Sunlight
glances off pie tins dancing in bare-bones
fig trees. A curious blue jay won't
mistake bed sheets whipping the clothesline
for thunderclap clap-snapping.
It's not raindrops landing on fault lines
in my garden I watch for—
something less essential,
something more.

Up in Smoke

He went missing Friday at halftime,
worst game of the season. No one liked him,
not even Coach who proclaimed
the kid lacks discipline.

Parents assured one another
that scrawny George or deaf Francis
couldn't have gotten even.

The makeshift Fire Department
braced themselves for dealing
with the boy's dad, a fire plug
who delayed the rescue squad with,

where's the fire? passing a flask
among men standing unevenly on
his ant pile yard. This gathering

a local would drive miles to
avoid. Uneven curtains parted,
closed. Grown men shuffled,
rolling then unrolling worn sleeves.

The evening wind carried
a whiff of scorched barbeque across
the pock-marked field. Hunger

vied with overwhelming relief
that good kids were accounted for—
an asthmatic, a pimply math whiz,
the stooped cross-eyed loner

who claimed he tracked fireflies,
let him help. A shy girl who
apologized if someone bumped her.

Playing With Fire

Easy, he shrugs, slitting the speared fish

below its bony frame from bottom to lower jaw,
anus to isthmus.

Flies abound in the dusk as he slowly fillets
into mirrored halves

what he wants. Must I note its entrails slump
onto a heel of bread?

The man comes alive as he stuns a slippery

one cutting patterns in the silky underworld.
I ask how he knows

my buff friend's friend. Those aquatic eyes
crush my skull. He grunts.

Huh? Don't come undone.   How far back
to civilization? Was that

blacktop numbered?   No house for miles.

He rubs together rough sticks that spit and
cackle at the sun.

Should I run?   No, don't second-guess this
bottom feeder.

He must have unstrung many a serious rod.
   Study the fire.

Track the knife. Don't catch his fiery gaze.

FOUR

The ultimate meaning to which all stories refer has two faces: the continuity of life, the inevitability of death.

—Italo Calvino

Fire!

4 a. m. Water thigh-deep,
living room-wide. I side-step axes
massive hands hip boots moving against the tide
lapping against our staircase
slapping my legs.
                      I buckle.

I find my daughter in my arms, laughing
all the way to the sidewalk where her daddy-long-leg
nudges the back of my knee.
                      I buckle again.

More laughter. As if helping her swing higher
higher. I turn her away from men riding hoses aiming at
nearby roofs. The homeless gawk.

All we had up in smoke.
A figure backlit by flames flaps like paper
from the top rung. Again I buckle. She points to a family of
plump caws along the power line.
Counts. Giggles.
                      Begins again.

Heading back from Padre Island

I see an olive-green helmet
in my headlights. No, a Kemp's Ridley
sea turtle! I swerve,

glance back.

Blind chance. What if I'd left
a moment later? Or earlier? I had to stop
for gas. What if

I'd blinked—

yawned, dozed, groped for the dial,
or reached back to shush my rarely cranky
sunburnt kids?

Disaster averted—

the moon head-lamping our path.
Aquarius spilling stars. No thump in the night.
My pulse revs,

downshifts.

Imagine

First attend your own funeral.
—Katherine Mansfield

I'm peeking in on my family now
that I've gone. The household prospers.
Each one sways like wheat along goldenrod
walls. There's room enough to stretch up
and out.

      How routine it had all seemed
long ago, all gunmetal grey, a sleek quiet
vacuum.

      Something in their grace says
there is only this world, this day. One half-
buried photo, small glimmer of what or when
I'd been, no sense or absence, nothing akin
to loss.

      As if what I touched folded
in like cinnamon in yellow cake batter.
Stir, erase.

Late Season

My fig tree weeps hard green tears for
eight-foot stalks that never knew burdensome corn.

Gracefully they slump over me,
their leaves gently nudging my shoulder.

Parched rain buckets beg
open-throated to a shameless, dry-eyed sky.

Crab apples dimpled as an old woman's derriere
plop on porous leaves. Two apple barrels

overflow with desiccated petals—Camelia,
Gardenia, Hydrangea—

scooped up in dawn heat for sachet packets.
Opaque grass crunches underfoot

like chipped ice. The emerald hose
poses a question mark around my Forsythia,

its point lost beneath a faucet that
cannot drip until pine trees no longer blaze.

I fling last week's bath water on my spindly
Widow's Lace, last surviving one in the parish,

outliving Mother, lovers, husbands,
and pray God takes me first.

Fading Light

Often you drift through
the sitting room then pass through a door

kept locked, a whoosh
rustling from your radiant blue down jacket.

You lay suffering in your bed for hours
as the wife sang, joyous

in church, glancing down the aisle for you.
I wonder if quiet logic

or doubt kept you home.
She found you around noon, half out of bed,

palm clutching your chest.
Spread across your contorted face: no god.

No, god? The doctor described suffering.
What comfort in that?

What she doesn't know is that you seized
my heart that first day.

Most, if not all, since.
Details knot the sheets, changing so little.

As I untangle them,
I can't offer what I do know of moaning.

Framed

after a Ray Metzker black-and-white photograph

Each passenger,
slumped,

unaware of an unblinking lens surveying
the passenger train.

Each photo meant to capture a flickering
on glass. A butterfly.

No gold-toothed grimace. No soft-focus
man awash in despair.

Wrinkled grace.
Patience.

Unrest

I cling to the left edge of the bed,
knees bent,

right foot resting on the ridge of my left toes.
How has it come to this, I wonder.

Inner ear taunting,
slip.

Wind shear hungry for
casualty,

a misplaced sigh

as whirling thoughts shake
my grip. I remain tacked in place

on a ledge slick with exhales.

To roll over would risk injury,
surrendering to vertigo's phantom twin.

Shift, I hear
then hold my breath.

Detritus

has made itself at home
in worn pockets of your faded jacket I love
to fall back on.

Tight rosebud of promise,
this burnt orange petal above the blood-stained
thorn. Then I clutch

a used Kleenex, its crinkle
conjuring individually wrapped butterscotch
wrappers coated

in crumbling peanut shells.
Why keep an empty Peanut M&M's bag or
last year's faded

gas receipt? Or this
short neck crossword pencil sporting a jaunty
eraser cap

I can't grasp. I'm one
penny shy of a nickel. No matter, here's
a sweaty bill

I smooth out on the counter,
defaced side down. Who would wish that
on Washington?

Keep the change. OK,
then, I'll settle on a tarnished quarter. No?
Twenty pennies?

Bedside Vigil

after André Kertész's "Melancholic Tulip"

At your bedside, a tulip wanes.
        Is it short on oxygen? Each papery

petal refuses to give in. Dare
        I mention its stamina? You fixate

on natural light like never before.
        Your round pasty face dissolves

like Alka Seltzer. How has it come
        to this? All these years, a strong

constitution, I recall. Which is
        what I'm left with, recollections.

Tennis matches. A fallen souffle.
        Putting our Collie down. *Oh, look,*

hon, your drinking straw holds
        sentry above a riot of pill bottles.

Can you not hear me? *Here, suck*
        some ice chips. Your eyes follow

dust motes. *A sprite?* What could
        I offer? That fixed gaze pulls taut

your chapped lips. You refuse
        a Vaseline-coated Q-tip. Endless

hours. A moon-faced wall clock
        snores softly at visiting hours.

Tabula rasa: white blanket tucks
        bleached sheets way too snug.

Nearby, a woman's *mea culpa.*
        A man objects to life support.

Whose will? Your ragged breath
    quivers, lifts, shakes free. Rests.

Man At Work

I step to the back of the empty elevator
as my boss bolts through its closing doors
then pivots to catch his polished reflection.

This space, an appropriated vanity box.
He leans in to study his four o'clock shadow,
inflating his cheeks like a tuba player mid-blow.

With Jim Carrey elasticity his giraffe tongue
buffs and sucks each tooth. His lips curl.

And for the final touch, repositions his manhood
in snug pants. A slave to appearance evermore.

I remain in his shadow, hands on hips, elbows
right-angled as if jutting from his pockets.
It's when he whirls from the lift, shoulders

squared, that I am noticed. Dowdy client?
No. Counsel or rainmaker? A nondescript
woman timeworn as our reception carpet.

I don't

appear the same in this mirror
as I do in others. In the one
near the hall closet I clothe myself
in composure. In this reflection,
I see myself self-conscious,
best sly sideways pose,
smile deep as my tummy tries to tuck,
posture-perfect, sloped shoulders thrust
back. That sucked-in sideways look
meant to suck others into
liking me without its likening
my slack demeanor. Bedroom mirrors
can reflect that as I prepare
a face to meet another's
expectation. Both mine and theirs
fade after that photo-op. And in the bath,
my relaxed glance is unprepared
for this aging countenance
I encounter first and last.
Saddened by the gulf
I find between those full-length gazes
and my peppy face
greeting the glassy door,
a windowpane's shadow or that
sheen from an elevator bank where I
step in and pulley a grave expression
to meet other masked
familiar faces.

Music of the Spheres

after a Da Camera "Inventors and Explorers" concert

I gaze into a telescope
that coaxes me toward Galileo's universe
as my weight leaves its grave position,
head and heart and balance flying and flaking like shooting stars
that seem to fall *up* and *away*,
never across, never
down to earth. Or ocean. I must rise with them,
little fragments of the self, bereft,
lightening the tenor of a cello lowing,
let go. What harm, then,
in shedding flecks oxidized by dread,
each blue haze clearing the narrow portal
I must pass through, this
make-shift hatch.

A Day So Pleasant

Oh, how we try to rearrange all that we see before us.
     —Jamaica Kincaid

I lie still so the grass can overtake
me. So flat so long
                    ants traverse the crook of my arm

before descending onto a few low blades. Milkweed waves
to monarchs as cattails tip
                    then shift

to deposit a ladybug near an ant pile. Mischief
air-borne.

A few ants lost in my arm hairs
wait for directions,
                    some signal it's time to move on.

A deer nibbles before ambling forward.

                    Come on, I coax,

as it nuzzles very near my toes. Which must not twitch.

I hold steady through dusk
as dew quilts my topside and grass prickles underneath.

Never have I lain so idle and not fallen
asleep. Never so content.

I could be the log at ease with its own decay.

                    At last, integrity.

Breathless In Portugal

Messejana sheep take me
as I am. Uphill downslide I traverse
sugar-cube cobblestone streets
caramelized by the sun. Oh Pot A Coffee
how I drank you in. Ribboning
lanes unravel downhill. At the bend
I lose myself in a skittish bleat.
A blue motorbike stalls then
sputters into card shuffling hiccups. Who
who knew, who, love, you would
perfect a disappearing act. Gambling
heart, when you leaned in, breathless,
I matched you, sheepish. Raised you ten.
Seven come eleven I got the bends.
Sleight of Hand. Oh tongue
that I never knew. I knew.

Gratitude

Thanks to my gracious poet friends—Kevin Prufer (2026 Texas Poet Laureate), David Meischen, Stan Crawford, Priscilla Frake, Rebecca Spears, and Sandi Stromberg—and countless others whose generosity, detachment, love of the craft, and unfiltered feedback remind this tortoise to not cross the highway. And when called for, to retract my flippers.

For my small cluster of unconditionals, immediate and extended. What brilliance and humor. And the swelling outer circle I have yet to meet, those that shimmer, share anecdotes, embellish. And humor me.

www.ingramcontent.com/pod-product-compliance
Lightning Source LLC
Chambersburg PA
CBHW030056170426
43197CB00010B/1549